||| | || ||||||| ||| |||| || ||| |||
I0117436

MARTHA'S VINEYARD NATURE GUIDE

SECOND EDITION

SYLVIA S. MADER

Design and Layout: Sylvia J. Kansfield
Illustrations: Kathleen Hagelston

Cover photo: ©Evelyn Jo Johnson

"Martha's Vineyard Nature Guide - Second Edition," by Sylvia S. Mader.
ISBN 978-1-949756-94-4(softcover).

Published 2020 by Virtualbookworm.com Publishing Company Inc., P.O. Box 9949,
College Station, TX 77842. Copyright 2020 by Sylvia S. Mader. All rights reserved.
No part of this publication may be reproduced, stored in a retrieval system, or
transmitted in any form or by any means, electronic, mechanical, recording or
otherwise, without the prior permission of Sylvia S. Mader.

Martha's Vineyard
Beautiful, special place
Magical, even spiritual

Lift your spirits
Visit the beaches,
Woods and wetlands

Keep the island beautiful
Leave only footprints!
Take out what you take in
Never leave any trash!

Poem by Sylvia S. Mader
Art: ©123RF/Paprika

Gay Head Cliffs

These cliffs are composed of clay and contain many fossilized plants and animals whose remains were deposited even before the last glacial advance, some nine or ten thousand years ago.

©Bruce M. Johnson

i

ACKNOWLEDGEMENTS

This edition of the *Martha's Vineyard Nature Guide* would not have been possible without the expertise and dedication of my longtime friend and assistant, Jo Johnson. Jo not only edited the manuscript, she also provided a large portion of the photos.

Many thanks also to my granddaughter Sylvia Kansfield for designing the beautiful cover and for laying out the pages in a competent and attractive manner. The drawings were beautifully done by my friend and longtime illustrator, Kathleen Hagelston.

The final product is due to the fine work of Virtualbookworm. com Publishing Company Inc. under the guidance of Bobby Bernshausen.

PREFACE

The Vineyard, because of its rural quality, offers a special opportunity to look at the natural world. This guide has been prepared to help you identify, understand, and enjoy the most commonly observed plants, animals, and natural areas of the island.

Along a roadside, you may encounter an open field, a dry woodland, or a wet woodland. At the beach, you will most likely first notice the shoreline and then an area of dunes, followed by a pond that serves as the location for a marsh. This guide will enable you to comprehend and appreciate each of these six habitats, along with their own mix of plants and animals suited to live in that area.

We suggest that you take this guide with you as you travel about the island. When you stop, notice the surroundings and decide which of the six habitats featured in the guide corresponds to where you are and compare the plants and any birds you see to the ones listed and described for that habitat. With little or no trouble, you will now be able to identify the most easily observed living things about you.

The author of this nature guide, Sylvia S. Mader, has also written the novel *A Water Lily Blooms*, which is partially set on the Vineyard. You can find out more about Sylvia at her website, sylviamader.com, where you can read the first chapter of her novel. It can be purchased at Vineyard bookstores, amazon.com, or virtualbookworm.com (publisher).

NANTUCKET SOUND

Atlantic Ocean

VINEYARD SOUND

ELIZABETH ISLANDS

Oak Bluffs

Tisbury (Vineyard Haven)

Edgartown

LCR

State Rd

West Tisbury

Chilmark

Aquinnah

MARTHA'S VINEYARD

★ Water Lily Pond on Lamber's Cove Rd (LCR)

NOMANS LAND

NORTH

0   5   10   15   20
Kilometres

UNITED STATES

iv

©Norman Einstein 10/14/2005, CC BY-SA 3.0

CONTENTS

ROADSIDES

OPEN FIELDS

Along a roadside there might be an open field that has few, if any, trees. This section of our guide lists and describes the wildflowers, vines, shrubs, and those trees most often seen here. It also describes birds that prefer open fields. 3

©pixphoto/123RF

WILDFLOWERS

WHITE FLOWERS

Queen Anne's Lace, Wild Carrot, or Bird's Nest
Daucus carota

Tall, slender plant; 1 to 4 ft. Leaves look like carrot leaves because they are much divided and finely cut. When crushed, they smell of carrot. The stem is covered with bristly hairs. The root also looks like a pale carrot. It is no wonder some believe that the garden carrot is a cultivated form of Queen Anne's Lace.

Each plant has a flat-topped cluster of tiny white, five-petaled flowers. Perhaps the cluster resembles Queen Anne's headdress. Then too, often there are two purple flowers in the center of the cluster. Therefore, another thought is that perhaps the purple flowers represent a drop of blood Queen Anne lost when tatting on a piece that resembles the flower cluster.

When the flowers have gone to seed, you may notice that the cluster curls to form a cup resembling a bird's nest. This accounts for the plant's third common name, Bird's Nest.

Blooms spring till fall.

Yarrow
Achillea millefolium

Tall, slender plant; 1 to 3 ft. Alternate leaves are lace-shaped and finely cut, as in ferns. If you run your fingers along the soft leaves and then sniff, you will notice a medicinal smell.

Tiny flowers, most often white but sometimes pink, occur in a flat-topped or rounded cluster that bears a superficial resemblance to Queen Anne's Lace.

Yarrow has been found to contain a blood-clotting substance, and it was used at times to stop bleeding.
Achilles is reported to have used it to heal the wounds of his soldiers, hence its botanical name.

Blooms late spring till early fall.

Hyssop-leaved
Thoroughwort or Boneset
Eupatorium hyssopifolium

A slender plant; 2 to 5 ft.
Long, light green, grasslike leaves in whorls of four or more, surround smaller leaves next to the stem. Herb doctors of old used the thoroughworts to help heal broken bones, thus this plant is some-times called Hyssop-leaved Boneset. The white flowers of this plant form fuzzy clusters at the ends of the branches.

Blooms late summer and fall.

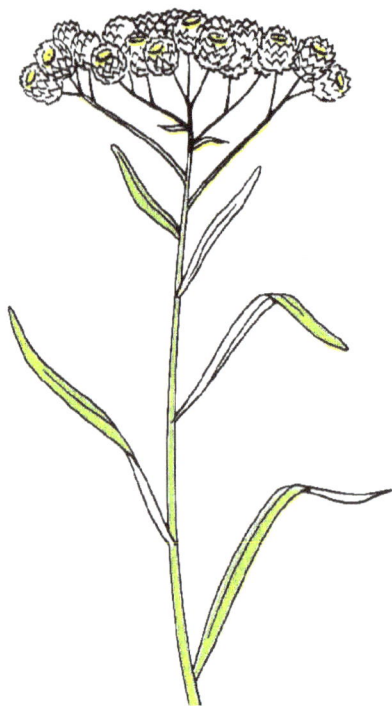

Sweet Everlasting
Gnaphalium obtusifolium

Tall, slender plant; 1 to 3 ft. Leaves are long and narrow, gray-green on top and wooly white on the underside. They give off a fragrance when crushed.

Although each globular flower is on its own short stalk, together they form a loose cluster at the top of the plant. Male flowers have a yellow center. Female flowers don't.

Blooms late summer and early fall.

Bladder Campion
Silene cucubalus

Moderate height plant; 8 to 18 in. The oppositely-placed, 3 to 4 in. leaves are rounded at the base and pointed at the tip. They attach directly to the stem.

White flowers with long stamens in the center are at the ends of many branches near the top of the main stem. The flower has five petals, but each one is so deeply notched that it looks like two petals.

The plant takes its common name from a unique feature: there is a swollen, bladder-shaped flower cup at the base of each flower. The flower cup is prominently veined with a tan or greenish color.

Blooms spring to late summer.

Pokeweed
Phytolacca americana

A stout, very vigorous and bushy plant; 4 to 10 ft. The leaves are large and veiny. Distinguishing characteristics of this plant are its vivid magenta stem and purple berries.

The small white flowers are borne in elongated clusters on stalks that have no leaves. At first, the berries are green, and then they become dark purple. Later in the season, you may find flowers at the lower portion of a cluster and berries at the tip of a cluster.

Young plants can be eaten as a vegetable, but once the stem has taken on the magenta color, all parts of the plant should be considered poisonous. The purple berries can be crushed into a bright purple juice that can be used as a dye or ink. The juice should be considered poisonous because it has a laxative and narcotic effect that can cause death.

Blooms summer and fall.

©Sara Tassan Mazzocco/123RF

YELLOW/ORANGE FLOWERS

©Ragesoss: CC BY-SA 3.0

Butterfly Weed or Pleurisy Root
Asclepias tuberosa

A tall, slender plant; 2 to 3 ft. The long, pointed leaves are placed alternate to one another on a rough, hairy stem.

The brilliant orange-colored flowers are particularly cherished on the Vineyard and it is especially advised NOT to pick them because there are fewer and fewer on the island. Each flower of the cluster has five curved-back petals arranged around five small upright petals. In the fall, the silky parachuted seeds are released from a graceful spindle-shaped pod.

Monarch butterflies and others are attracted to and feed off these plants and this explains their common name. They are also called Pleurisy Root because the Native Americans chewed the tough underground stem as a cure for pleurisy, a lung condition.

Blooms early summer until early fall.

Black-eyed Susan
Rudbeckia serotina

A slender, non-branched plant; 1 to 3 ft. Rough, hairy, long narrow or oval leaves are placed alternately on a rough, hairy stem.

The 2 to 3 in. wide flowers have bright yellow petals that surround a dark-brownish center. This feature accounts for the flower's common name.

Blooms summer and fall.

Butter-and-Eggs
Linaria vulgaris

Tall, slender plant; 1 to 3 ft. with numerous thin leaves that are placed alternately around the stem.

The snapdragon-like flowers grow in an elongated cluster at the end of a stalk. Long, pale yellow petals surround an orange-yellow center, and this accounts for the common name of the plant.

Blooms in the spring and summer.

St. John's Wort
Hypericum perforatum

A branched plant; 2 to 5 ft. The small, numerous, oblong leaves are placed opposite to one another on a slender stem.

Bright yellow flowers are arranged in a small cluster at the end of each branch. Each star-shaped flower is about 1 in. across and has five spreading petals, with black dots toward the edges. Settlers gathered these plants on St. John's Eve, June 24th, and hung them in the doors of their homes to ward off evil spirits. The word wort simply means a plant.

Blooms summer and early fall.

Wild Indigo
Baptisia tinctoria

A very branched plant; 1 to 3 ft.
Each of the alternate leaves has three
oval leaflets. The stem and leaves are
bluish-green when the plant is living,
but they turn black when the plant is cut
and dried. When steeped in water and
allowed to ferment, the leaves yield a
blue dye. This accounts for its common
and scientific names.

The yellow pea-like flowers are in
clusters at the end of the branches.

Blooms summer and early fall.

Goldenrod
Solidago

Tall, slender plant; 1 to 5 ft. Leaves are
elongated but vary in length and width
according to the type of goldenrod.

All of the goldenrods have yellow
flowers in various types of clusters.
Although most people can recognize
goldenrod, even botanists hesitate to
distinguish one type from another. The
Canada Goldenrod (*Solidago canadensis*)
is one of the most common tall goldenrods, with a distinctive plum-like cluster.

Contrary to popular belief, goldenrods
do NOT cause the allergic symptoms of
hay fever; these are often caused by
Ragweed. In contrast, many types of
goldenrod are used in herbal medicine,
and this accounts for their scientific
name, *Solidago*, which means "whole"
or "to make whole" in Latin.

Blooms summer and fall.

BLUE FLOWERS

Chicory or Blue Sailors
Cichorium intybus

A tall plant; 2 to 5 ft. There are large dandelion-like leaves at the base of the main stalk of the chicory, but its other leaves are smaller and oblong. Leaves are attached alternately, directly to the stem, which gives off short branches.

At any time, there are usually a few bright blue flowers scattered along the stem and branches. The petals are square-tipped and fringed. This plant was brought from Europe because the stout root could be roasted, ground, and used as a substitute for coffee.

It is still sometimes used in this manner, but more often it is added to coffee mixtures to enhance the flavor. The other common name, Blue Sailors, comes from a legend about a sailor who went to sea, leaving his beloved to wander along the highway waiting for his return. The gods changed her to this plant, which still haunts the roadsides and has sailor-blue flowers.

©Oxana Gilman/123RF

11

Virginia Creeper or Woodbine
Parthenocissus quinquefolia

A beautiful vine found climbing along roadside fences, but also up and into many trees. It climbs by means of tendrils that reach out and end in small adhesive discs. Each leaf consists of usually five pointed and toothed leaflets that are arranged like an open fan. (Some people confuse Virginia Creeper with Poison Ivy, but notice on pp. 18–19 that the Poison Ivy leaf has three leaflets only.) The leaves turn a beautiful red in the fall.

Small, greenish flowers are clustered at the ends of branches in the spring. In the fall, they become dark blue berries, about 1/4 in. in diameter. The berries should be considered poisonous.

Flowers in spring. Berries in fall.

©Dejan Lazarevic/123RF

Bittersweet
Celastrus scandens

A woody vine that climbs on any support available, such as a fence or stone wall. The oval leaves are light green and toothed.

The yellowish-green flowers are small and inconspicuous. However, the flowers are followed by dull orange capsules, about 3/8 in. in diameter. When mature in early to late fall, they open to expose bright scarlet seeds. Although some animals can eat the berries, the berries are poisonous for humans.

Flowers in spring. Berries in fall.

©Lianem/123RF

Pasture Rose
Rosa carolina

A very branched shrub, 6 in. to 3 ft. The leaves usually have five to nine egg-shaped leaflets, sharply toothed. Distinctive characteristics are the sharp, slender, straight thorns that grow only where the leaves join the prickly, often red, stem.

The pink flowers, which are about 2 in. wide and have five petals, occur singly. They have a delightful smell. In the fall, the flowers become red berry-like fruits, known as hips. Pasture Rose hips are sometimes steeped in hot water to make a tea or used in jellies and candies. Like all hips, they are a rich source of vitamin C.

Flowers in spring. Hips in fall.

©D. Gordon E. Robertson: CC BY-SA 3.0

ROADSIDES

Muliflora Rose
Rosa multiflora

A rambling rose that sometimes trails along or arches over. The leaves usually have seven to nine oval, toothed leaflets that occur in pairs, except for the terminal one.

The numerous small white flowers, each with five petals, occur in a variably shaped, loose cluster. In the fall, each flower becomes a typical red rose hip.

Flowers in spring. Hips in fall.

©Σ64: CC BY 3.0

Sumacs
Rhus

Treelike shrubs; 2 to 12 ft. Each leaf has numerous leaflets. In Dwarf Sumac (*Rhus copallinum*), the branches, leaves, and flower stalks have minute ash-colored hairs, and the main leaf rib between the leaflets has extensions called wings. These features are lacking in Smooth Sumac (*Rhus glabra*), whose toothed leaves are white on the underside. The sumacs provide some of the Vineyard's most colorful foliage as their leaves turn from bright orange to dark crimson in the fall.

The yellow-green flowers appear in May or June. In Dwarf Sumac, they form a yellow-green pointed cluster; and in Smooth Sumac they take the shape of a pyramid. Each flower becomes a red berry in the fall.

Both Dwarf and Smooth Sumac are not poisonous. In fact, the berries are edible and can be used to make a pink lemonade or can be boiled to make a tea. Poisonous sumac (not shown here) is not only inedible, but it also causes a rash if touched. It is easy to tell poisonous sumac from edible sumac.

Poisonous sumac bears white berries in a drooping cluster as opposed to the red, upright, conelike cluster of berries of edible sumac. There is some Poison Sumac (*Rhus vernix*) on the island, but it is more likely to be found in swampy areas.

Flowers in spring. Berries in fall.

Dwarf Sumac

Homer Edward Price: CC BY-SA 2.0

Smooth Sumac

Eric Hunt: CC BY-SA 4.0

POISON IVY

Poison Ivy
Rhus radicans

This is a plant you need to be able to recognize in all its forms because it causes an itching and weeping rash to many who touch it. The alternately placed leaves have three leaflets, and these are often lobed. In the spring, the small, variable leaves are dark red. In the summer, they are dark green and frequently shiny. In the fall, the leaves are colored either red or yellow, and they contrast prettily with the white berries that appear at this time.

Poison Ivy can be an erect shrub, 2 to 7 ft. tall, or a vine that climbs on stone walls and trees. The stem is smooth and is rarely branched. It may be darkened in old plants.

Poison Ivy flowers in the late spring. Each flower has five yellowish to greenish petals, and they occur in clusters where the leaves come off the stem. Consequently, in the fall, the whitish, 1/4 inch round berries are also in clusters. Many species of wildlife eat these berries.

BE CAREFUL NOT TO TOUCH ANY PART OF THIS PLANT IN ANY SEASON BECAUSE IT IS ALWAYS POISONOUS.

Spring

©Unitysphere/123RF

ROADSIDES

Summary

©Cramyourspam: CC BY-SA 4.0

Fall

Famartin: CC BY-SA 4.0

Red Cedar
Juniperus virginiana

A small, spirelike evergreen tree that usually grows to less than 20 feet. The older branches are smooth and easy to run your hand along; the new branches are sharp and prickly. This is due to a difference in the type of leaf. On older branches, the greenish to reddish-brown leaves are scalelike and adhere closely. On new branches, the leaves are needle-shaped and a little lighter in color.

The hard fruit is light blue and berrylike. It remains on the tree during the winter and is highly prized by birds. The wood is soft and fragrant. It may be used to line a closet as protection against moths.

©Evelyn Jo Johnson

Black Cherry
Prunus serotina

A small tree (or small shrub); 10 to 80 ft.
The very thin, alternate oval leaves are bright
green above and paler below; they are sharply
toothed and come to an abrupt point. Although
the bark on the trunk is rough and black, the
branches are smooth and grey or reddish.

The small white flowers form an upright cluster
that has the shape of a cylinder. Each flower has
five round, spreading petals. The flowers are
followed by dark red to nearly black cherries.
Each cherry is on a small stalk attached to the
main stalk of a now drooping cluster. They are
sour but will make a good jam or jelly.
The pits themselves should be removed and not
swallowed because they are poisonous.

Blooms in spring. Cherries in fall.

Russian Olive
Elaeagnus angustifolia

A shrub of variable height. The alternate leaves
are long and slender, with a rounded tip. They
have an olive-green upper surface, but the un-
dersurface is silver and shiny. From a distance,
you will see flashes of white whenever the wind
exposes the undersides of the leaves.

Small yellow flowers produce a yellow fruit that
is shaped like an olive. This plant is not native to
the Vineyard; it is an ornamental plant that has
escaped to the roadside.

Blooms in spring. Fruits in fall.

BIRDS

All birds selected are the common birds on the Vineyard that are most apt to be seen by the summertime visitor.

Hawks

The Red-tailed Hawk (*Buteo jamaicensis*) is one of the largest hawks found on the Vineyard. With a husky body designed for strength and not speed, it is apt to be seen soaring over open fields in search of prey that it can catch and hold with sharp claws and tear into pieces with its sharp beak. Only the adult has the distinctive reddish tail. While the wings are darkly colored above, the underbody is white. There is a belly band of dark streaks.

The Marsh Hawk, or Northern Harrier, (*Circus cyaneus*) is slimmer than the Red-tailed Hawk, and it rarely soars. Instead, it is usually seen flapping leisurely or gliding close to the ground, over meadows and marshes. The Marsh Hawk has a dark body but a white rump patch, a distinguishing characteristic. Both males and females are whitish below, but the female has heavy brown streaking on the breast.

The Sparrow Hawk, or American Kestrel, (*Falco sparverius*) is smaller still and faster than the other two. It eats mice and insects, sometimes caught on the wing. The back and tail are rust red, and there are double black stripes on a white face. The male has blue-gray, long pointed wings that move rapidly in flight. You can find this hawk near houses. Its cry is a shrill "killy-killy-killy".

Red-tailed Hawk ©Greg Hume: CC BY-SA 3.0

Sparrow Hawk ©Greg Hume: CC BY-SA 3.0

Marsh Hawk ©Steve Byland/123RF

Crow
Corvus brachyrhynchos

A large, black bird that is readily identified by its familiar flapping flight and noisy "caw" call. Crows are usually seen in flocks except during nesting season.

American Crow ©Mdf: CC BY-SA 3.0

Goldfinch
Carduelis tristis

Small birds that are often called the Wild Canary because of their yellow coloring. They like thistle and sunflower seeds and are often seen at feeders containing these seeds. In the spring and summer, the male is bright yellow with a black cap, wings, and lower tail; the upper rump is white. These birds have a characteristic roller coaster flight and a "per-chic-oree" call on the wing.

American Goldfinch ©Mdf: CC BY-SA 3.0

Barn Swallow ©Malene Thyssen: CC BY-SA 4.0

Tree Swallow ©Iiii I I I: CC BY-SA 4.0

Swallows

Swallows: slender bodies and long, pointed wings; often seen in flocks or perching in long rows on rooftops and wires. Barn Swallows (*Hirundo rustica*) have a dark, steel-blue body above and cinnamon underparts. They are the only swallow with a deeply forked tail. They nest in barnlike buildings and under rock ledges. Tree Swallows (*Tachycineta bicolor*), which usually nest in trees, are dark, glossy blue-green above and white below.

Like other swallows, both are fast and graceful gliders.

Robin ©Kristof vt: CC BY-SA 3.0
Turdus migratorius

Male Robins have a gray-brown body, but a darker head and tail. While the full breast is orange-red, the lower belly is white. Female Robins are duller, and the young have speckled breasts. This is one of the first birds that most people learn to identify. They are frequently seen on people's lawns where they feed on worms. Listen carefully for their "cheeri-up, cheeri-up" song.

Starling ©Fred Hsu: CC BY-SA 3.0
Sturnus vulgaris

In summer, these birds are black with a yellow bill. They can be distinguished from other black birds by their short, square tail; stocky body; and short, pointed wings. These birds were introduced to the United States from Europe about a hundred years ago, and since then have helped cause a decline in native bird population sizes. Their bold and aggressive behavior helps them acquire nesting sites and food at the expense of local birds.

Rock Dove ©Coroiu Octavian/123RF

Mourning Dove ©Don Debold: CC BY-SA 2.0

Doves

Doves are small-headed, short-legged birds that bob their heads and coo while walking. Rock Doves (*Columba livia*) are the common pigeon seen particularly in towns and on the ferries. Typically, there is a white rump, dark head, and dark bands on wings and tail. The call is a soft "coo-cuk-cuk-cuk-coooo." Mourning Doves (*Zenaida macroura*) have a trimmer body and longer tail than Rock Doves. The body is fawn brown, and in flight, you can see outer white tail feathers. The call is a mournful cooing.

Bobwhite
Colinus virginianus

A small, mottled, reddish-brown bird that is usually found near the ground. Males have a white throat and a white eye stripe. These areas are light brown in females. The males have the distinctive "bob-bob-white" call in the spring and a "hoy" call year-round.

©BS Thurner Hoff: CC BY-SA 3.0

Ring-necked Pheasant
Phasianus colchicus

These are large, stout birds, unmistakable because of their long, pointed tails. Males have a dark green head, with red eye patches and short black plumes.

©Piotr Krzeslak/123RF

Often there is a broad white neck ring. The body and wings are a shiny bronze, speckled with brown and black. Females are sandy brown and lack the coloration of the male, although they have the same general shape. These birds fly only for short distances and generally run to escape danger.

© pixphoto/123RF

On the Vineyard, country roads often take us from open fields to woodlands, the topic of the next section.

ROADSIDES

DRY WOODLANDS

Along a roadside, there may be a dry woodland that contains pine and oak trees, beneath which Huckleberry and Blueberry bushes grow. This section of our guide lists and describes those trees typical of the Vineyard as well as birds that prefer dry woodland areas.

31

©Evelyn Jo Johnson

TREES

White Oak

Oak Trees
Quercus

White Oak courtesy of the Vineyard Gazette, vineyardgazette.com. ©Vineyard Gazette, all rights reserved. Photograph by Mark Alan Lovewell.

Oak trees are deciduous trees; that is, they lose their leaves in the winter. They all have acorns, which produce another tree when planted. The best way to get acquainted with the island's oak trees is to divide them into two major groups: the White Oaks and the Black Oaks.

The white oaks include the **White Oak** (*Quercus alba*) pictured above and the **Post Oak** (*Quercus stellata*). They both have alternate leaves with rounded lobes. The kernels of the acorns are usually sweet. They take their name from their pale bark and not from the leaves, which are dark green above and paler green below.

Post Oak

The Post Oak is a slower growing species, and its wood is strong and resistant to rot; therefore it is often used in fencing. Young Post Oak trees are likely found in new growth near stone walls originally built to confine sheep. If left undisturbed, the tree can become as large as the White Oak in the photo above.

Black Oak

Scarlet Oak

Black Oak ©Willow: CC BY-SA 3.0

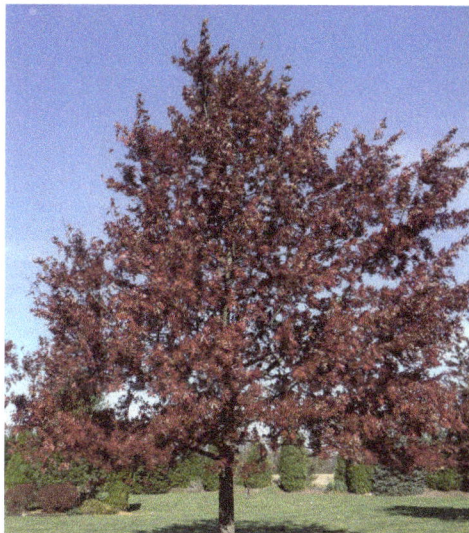

Scarlet Oak ©Famartin: CC BY-SA 4.0

The Black Oaks have alternate leaves with bristle tips. The members of this group on the Vineyard are the **Black Oak** (*Quercus velutina*), the **Scarlet Oak** (*Quercus coccinea*), and the **Scrub Oak** (*Quercus ilicifolia*). Their acorns have a bitter taste. Although the bark on young stems is smooth and still only dark brown, it soon becomes rough and black. The mature leaves are dark green above and coppery green below. The Scarlet Oak has brilliant coloring in the fall; the Scrub Oak is smaller than the other two.

There are commonly uneven, light green patches adhering to the bark of all oak trees and even fuzzy, green growths dangling from some of their branches. These are lichens, each of which is a unique combination of algal cells (green) and fungal cells (colorless) that produce their own food and do the tree no harm. Their presence indicates that the island is relatively free of air pollution; lichens are not seen in areas where there is polluted air.

Scrub Oak

Pine Trees

Pinus

Pitch Pine

Red Pine

©Famartin: CC BY-SA 3.

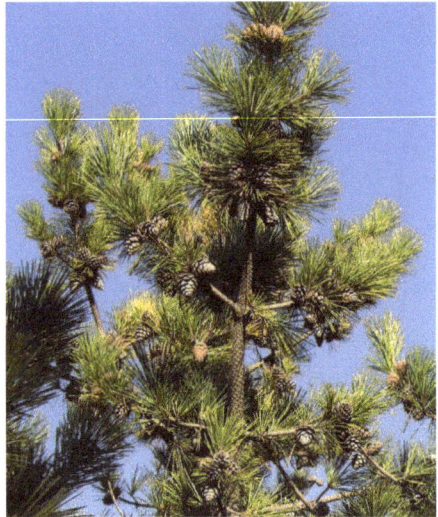

©Rhododendrites: CC BY-SA 4.0

Pine trees are evergreen trees, with needlelike leaves and woody cones. Mature female cones open up to release seeds.

The **Pitch Pine** (*Pinus rigida*), the only native pine tree, is one of the most common trees on the Vineyard. The stiff needles of this pine tree are in clusters of three and have a length of 3 to 5 in. The thick bark is very rough and deeply furrowed, with loose, dark reddish-brown scales. The cone is 2 to 3 in. long, and somewhat egg-shaped, without a stem. There are sharp prickles on the tip of each cone scale.

The **Red Pine** (*Pinus resinosa*) tree has 3 to 6 in. long, flexible needles in clusters of two. The reddish-brown bark has shallow, flat ridges separating into thin, flaky scales. The cone is 2 in. long, without a stem, and the cone scales lack prickles. This type pine tree was planted in the State Forest down-island because it grew well in its sandy soil and was believed to be resistant to infections. However, this did not prove to be the case and almost all the Red Pine trees in the State Forest succumbed to a fungal infection and have been replaced with White Pine (*Pinus strobus*) or Norway Spruce (*Picea abies*).

White Pine

©Brian Lasenby/123RF

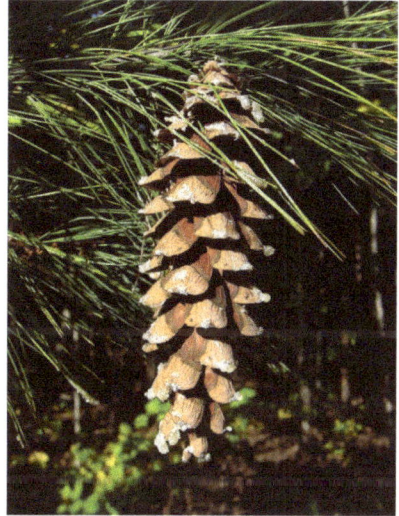
©Keith Kanoti, Maine Forest Svc: CC BY-SA 3.0

The **White Pine**, recognized by having five needles in a cluster, is common to the east coast and will grow in almost any soil as long as sunlight is plentiful. It's found in dense lowland forests and on high mountaintops. It is popular in suburban neighborhoods because it can grow quickly, even several feet a year, and could last in urban areas for 100 years.

One of its best qualities is to serve as a windbreak, but it also blocks the line of sight because it attains great height within a short period of time. White pine trees can reach a height of 40 feet within 20 years.

Pine trees typically have both male and female flowers. Having male flowers on each tree assures that following pollination, female flowers will produce seed-bearing cones. Their seeds are a source of food for small animals, including various birds.

Sassafras Trees

Sassafras albidum

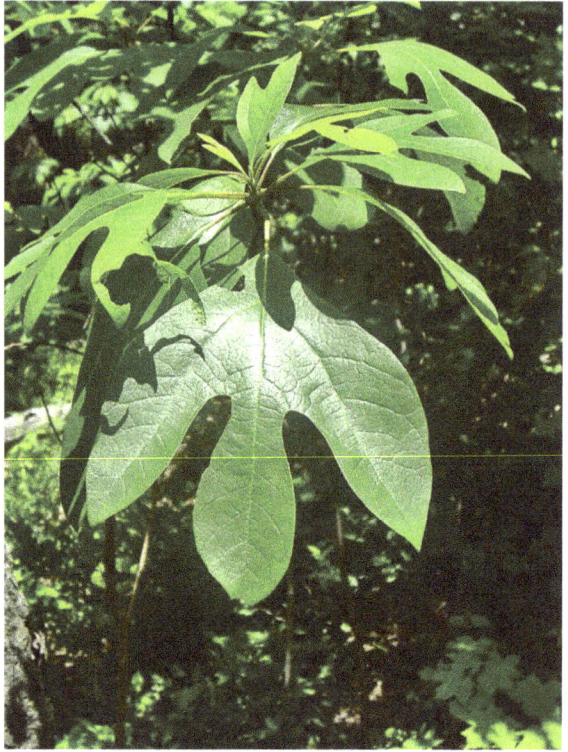

©Wowbobwow12: CC BY-SA 3.0

This is a small-to-medium sized, deciduous tree that has three different shapes of leaves—some are ovate (egg-shaped), others are mitten-shaped (both right- and left-handed), and still others are three-lobed. The reddish-brown bark is stout, rugged, and deeply grooved.

Sassafras trees are well known because the bark and root can be used to make sassafras tea. The berrylike fruit is dark blue and shiny. Each is attached to a bright red stalk.

SHRUBS

Huckleberry and Blueberry Bushes

These shrubs are frequently seen as low, bushy growth beneath oak trees. The alternate leaves are small, oval, and slightly rough to touch. In the Black Huckleberry (*Gaylussacia*) there are resin dots on the leaves. Such dots are lacking in the Blueberry (*Vaccinium*), whose twigs have raised areas called warts. In both, the slender green-to-reddish twigs sometimes zigzag.

Both have small pale flowers that are bell-shaped. These become round berries that have a star-shaped pattern on the upper tip. In Huckleberry bushes the berries tend to be a darker blue, while in Blueberry bushes they tend to have a white powder.

Flowers in summer. Berries ripen from June to September.

Huckleberry

Lowbush Blueberry

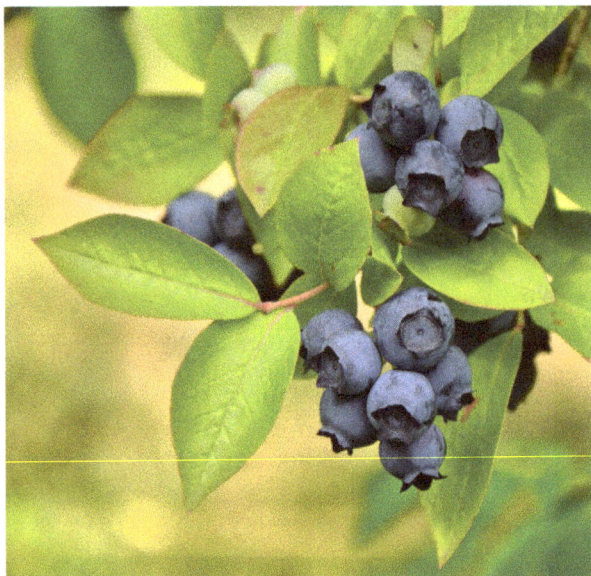

©Malgorzata Slusarczyk/123RF

Highbush Blueberry
Vaccinium corymbosum

This bush can grow to 10 ft., in which case the bark is usually light gray and rather flaky. Small oval leaves are arranged alternately on short, wart-covered, slender branches that sometimes zigzag. In the fall, the green leaves become a flaming red to a dark maroon-red.

The small, attractive, bell-shaped flowers occur in clusters during June and July. The berries that follow are round, with a star-shaped pattern on the outer tip. Blueberries often have a white powder.

Flowers in summer. Berries ripen from June to September.

BIRDS

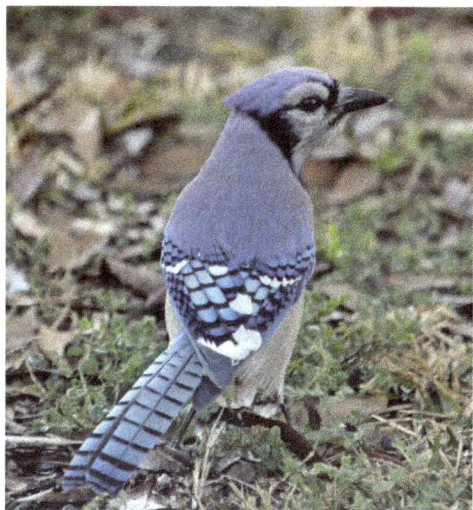

©Dick Daniels: CC BY-SA 3.0

Blue Jay
Cyanocitta cristata

Blue jays are large, crested birds with blue wings and tail, both of which have black barring and white patches. Beneath, the underparts are whitish with a black bib. The most common call is a piercing "jay, jay, jay."

Rufous-sided Towhee
Pipilo erythrophthalmus

Rufous-sided towhees are very common birds on Martha's Vineyard and could be considered the Vineyard's own special bird. Males have black upperparts, but beneath, chestnut sides border a white breast. White wing patches and white tail edges are seen in flight. While females are brown above, they have the same under-coloring as the males. The song of these birds sounds like "drink-your-tea-ee-ee-ee-ee." The call is a slurred "chewink."

©Bill Thompson/US Fish & Wildlife Service, Public Domain

White-breasted nuthatch
©www.naturespicsonline.com: CC BY-SA 2.5

Red-breasted nuthatch
©Cephas: CC BY-SA 3.0

Nuthatches
Sitta

The White-breasted Nuthatch (*Sitta carolinensis*) has a black cap and blue-gray back above whitish underparts, while the Red-breasted Nuthatch (*Sitta canadensis*) is similar except for reddish underparts. The White-breasted rather than the Red-breasted is apt to be seen in summer. These birds are most often seen on trees, where they work in a head-down position, looking for insects under the bark. Both have a twangy nasal call of "yank-yank"; their song sounds like "who-who-who-who-who," all run together.

Black-capped Chickadee
Parus atricapillus

These are small, plump birds, with white cheeks but black caps and bibs. Their high, clear song is a slow "chick-a-dee-dee-dee."

©Mdf assumed: CC BY-SA 3.0

©cbgrfx123: CC BY-SA 4.0

Brown Thrasher
Toxostoma rufum

The long tail is an identifying characteristic of the Brown Thrasher. The upper body is a solid, bright rusty color, but the whitish breast is streaked. Sitting where it can be seen, the Brown Thrasher sings a song rich in quality, but with many repeated phrases.

©Steve Byland/123RF

Catbird
Dumetella carolinensis

The Catbird is plain dark gray, with a black cap and a long black tail, often cocked. There is a chestnut color beneath the tail. The song is a mixture of various sounds, especially because these birds are good mimics —they copy the songs of other birds. Even so, you can tell the bird is a Catbird because every once in a while you will hear a catlike mew.

©Hari Krishnan: CC BY-SA 4.0

Cardinal
Cardinalis cardinalis

Both male and female Cardinals have pointed crests and loud, whistled songs, but only the male is bright red with a black face. The slightly smaller female is light reddish-tan. Often seen at bird feeders, they nest in trees and shrubs around houses.

DRY WOODLANDS

41

Flicker
©Marie-Ann Daloia/123RF

Downy woodpecker
©Wolfgang Wander: CC BY-SA 3.0

Hairy woodpecker
©Mdf: CC BY-SA 3.0

Flicker
Colaptes auratus

The Flicker is a big bird with a brown-barred back and spotted underparts. A sharp bill allows it to hammer loudly on trees and metal objects. However, these birds feed on the ground, eating ants and other insects. There is a red patch on the back of the neck and a black crescent bib on the front. You can see golden feathers under the wings and tail in flight. The most common call is a loud and rapid "wik-wik-wik."

Woodpecker
Picoides

Both the Downy Woodpecker (*Picoides pubescens*) and the Hairy Woodpecker (*Picoides villosus*) are found pecking on trees in the woodlands of the Vineyard. Their breast and back are white, but the face and wings show both white and black markings. Males have a red patch on the back of the head. The Downy Woodpecker is smaller than the Hairy Woodpecker.

OTHER ANIMALS

Many people are interested to know if there are any dangerous animals on Martha's Vineyard. We are happy to report that there are none. For example, there are no poisonous snakes and no large animals that would attack humans. There are deer to be seen occasionally by the lucky observer and, unfortunately, skunks sometimes make their presence known in an unsavory manner.

ROADSIDES

WET WOODLANDS

Occasionally along a roadside, there is a wet woodland that contains trees and bushes and ferns that require a ready supply of water. This section of our guide lists and describes those plants and birds that prefer a wet woodland area.

©Evelyn Jo Johnson

TREES

©Famartin: CC BY-SA 4.0

Red Maple
Acer rubrum

The Red Maple tree has the typical maple leaf, but note the sharp angle between the leaf lobes. Looking closely, you will notice the red on the stems; even so, this maple takes its name from the brilliant fall color of the leaves. Its winged seeds occur in clusters on long stalks in May or early June. Red Maple trees are most apt to be found in wooded areas where the soil is wet. Another name for these trees is Swamp Maple.

©Famartin: CC BY-SA 4.0

Beetlebung or Tupelo Tree

Nyssa sylvatica

A moderately-sized tree, 20 to 60 ft., with horizontal or drooping branches. The bark is deeply corrugated and gray on older trees. The pointed, alternate, oval leaves are dark olive-green on the upper surface, but paler below. They turn a beautiful dark scarlet in the early fall, making the trees easy to identify at this time. Small greenish flowers, borne two or three to a cluster, become blue-black berries in the fall. Off the Vineyard, these trees are often called Tupelo trees, but on the Vineyard, they are called Beetlebung trees. The name beetlebung refers to beetles, or mallets, that were made from the tree's wood and used to drive bungs, or stoppers, into whale oil barrels. As you most likely know, the Vineyard was an important center for whaling in the 1800s.

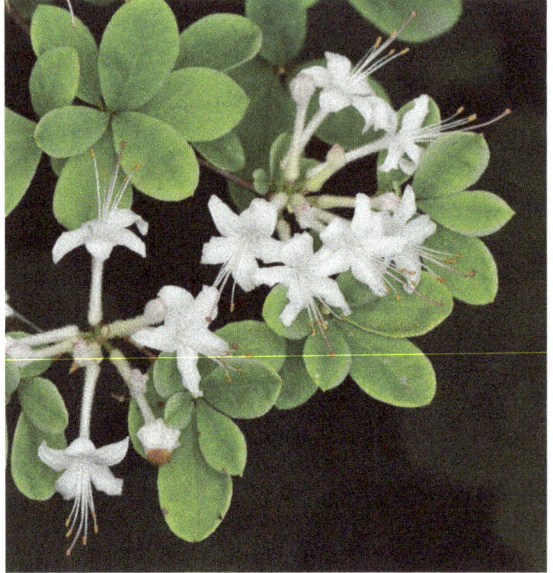

©HorsePunchKid: CC BY-SA 4.0

Swamp Azalea or Clammy Azalea

Rhododendron viscosum

An 8 ft. shrub that has twigs growing in characteristic whorls.

The white, 1.5 in. trumpet-shaped flowers have a heavy cinnamon-like smell and give off a sticky substance. The flowers become dried, brown seed capsules that remain during winter and look like dried brown flowers.

Flowers early spring to summer. Seed capsules in fall.

©Fritzflohrreynolds: CC BY-SA 3.0

©Amelia Martin/123RF

Shadbush or Juneberry
Amelanchier

These are shrubs or small trees that grow in clumps. The 2 to 4 in. oval leaves are alternate and finely toothed.

Showy flowers, with five long petals, form fragrant clusters in the spring, often before the leaves are out. The plant is called Shadbush because the flowers appear about the time the Shad migrate upstream to spawn. The other name for this plant, Juneberry, is also appropriate because the flowers become berries as early as June. Although they resemble blueberries, they tend to be reddish-purple in color and a little plumper.

Flowers early in spring. Berries in summer and fall.

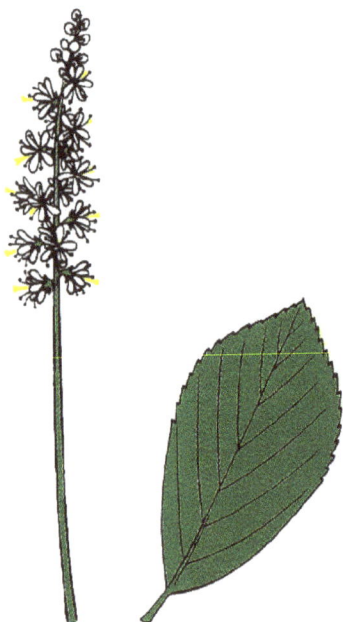

©KENPEI: CC BY-SA 3.0

Sweet Pepperbush

Clethra alnifolia

A 3 to 10 ft. shrub that grows in wet places and often forms dense thickets. The oval leaves are toothed only toward their tips.

Small white flowers form a very fragrant terminal cluster with a spicy odor.

Flowers summer and early fall.

VINES

©Evelyn Jo Johnson

Wild Grapes
Vitis

Grape vines have thick, thornless stems that climb by means of tendrils. The large heart-shaped leaves are coarsely toothed and often lobed.

The small, fragrant flowers are green or greenish-yellow. They are borne in compact clusters opposite the leaves and may appear in the spring as the leaves begin to expand. These become purple, blue, black, or amber grapes that have few seeds and are juicy. They can be used to make grape juice, jams, or jellies.

FERNS

Bracken Fern

Cinnamon Fern

Sensitive Fern

Ferns are plants usually with very large leaves that are very apt to be found growing on the floor of a woodland. In the spring, when ferns first begin growing, the leaves are in a tight coil known as a fiddlehead. As the head bends backward, the leaves unfold. Each leaf of a fern contains many leaflets.

Three common ferns are the Bracken (*Pteridium aquilinum*), Sensitive (*Onoclea sensibilis*), and Cinnamon (*Osmunda cinnamomea*) Ferns. The Bracken Fern will grow in dry and wet places, while the other two types prefer only damp places. The Sensitive Fern takes its name from its inability to survive early frosts. In midsummer, it sends up a leaf that appears to bear dark green berries. These contain the spores by which this fern reproduces itself. The Cinnamon Fern takes its name from a similar structure that contains bright cinnamon-colored spikes.

BIRDS

©Walter Siegmund: CC BY-SA 3.0

Red-winged Blackbird
Agelaius phoeniceus

This medium-tailed bird is common along ponds, lakes, and marshes. The glossy-black males have bright red shoulder patches edged with yellow. Unless the male is flying, the red patch can be hard to see. Females resemble big, streaky sparrows, but have a more pointed bill.

Males have a gurgling "cong-lo-reee" song, ending in a trill. The most common call is a "chack" note.

©Daniel D'Auria: CC BY-SA 4.0

Canada Goose
Branta canadensis

These large, web-footed birds are most often seen in flocks, honking as they fly in a V formation overhead. The black head and neck, with a distinctive white chin strap, make these birds easy to identify. Note the large, dark wings when the bird is flying and also the white beneath the tail and across the rump.

The call is a deep "honk-a-lonk" in larger birds.

WET WOODLANDS

53

Great Blue Heron ©Marie-Ann Daloia/123RF   Snowy Egret ©Brian Lasenby/123RF

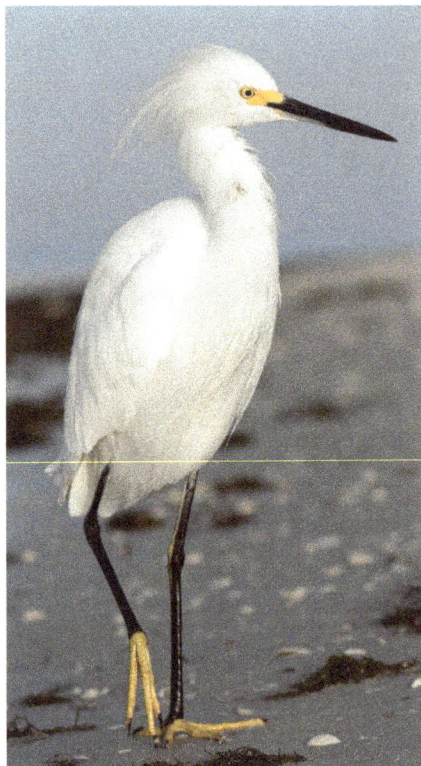

Herons and Egrets

Herons and egrets are wading birds that have long legs and neck, and a pointed bill for gathering food in shallow water. They commonly stand with the neck bent in an S shape. The Great Blue Heron (*Ardea herodias*) is a large gray-blue bird with a whitish head. A black stripe extends above the eye onto the head, and the neck has a front streak of black. The Snowy Egret (*Egretta thula*) has a white body, slender black bill, yellow eyes, black legs, and bright yellow feet.

©Richard Bartz: CC BY-SA 2.5

Mallard

Anas platyrhynchos

The Mallard is a familiar bird on freshwater ponds and also in salt marshes in the winter. They rarely dive and, instead, they feed by tipping, tail-up. They usually jump to take off and rarely need a running start. The male of this species is easy to identify because the head and neck are metallic green. There is also a white color line above the chestnut breast. The female has a nondistinctive, mottled appearance, but there are white bars before and after a blue patch on the wing. The female quacks when she calls; the male uses reedy notes.

BEACHES
SHORELINES

Only the remains of seaweeds and various seashells are most often found on a beach. This section of our guide identifies some of the birds that prefer the beach habitat and also the most common types of seashells found there.

57

©Robhillphoto/123RF

SEAWEED

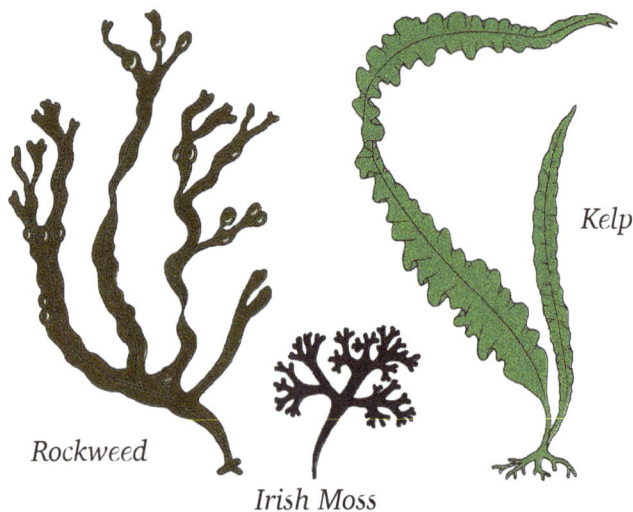

Rockweed

Irish Moss

Kelp

Rockweed ©Evelyn Jo Johnson

When you walk along a beach you often notice a dark line running parallel to the water's edge. Here you will find, among other things, remains of plants known as algae. Algae are named for their color, and you will probably notice brown, red, and green algae. Some of these algae are long and stringy; some have many branches, and some have blades that seem like broad leaves. The yellow capsules are air bladders that keep this alga afloat.

BIRDS

Herring Gull ©Kurt Kulac: CC BY-SA 4.0

Great Black-backed Gull ©Spinus Nature Photography: CC BY-SA 3.0

Gulls
Larus

Gulls (sometimes called seagulls) are the large birds that one often sees at the water's edge or following the ferry in order to get food, even out of passengers' hands. Two types of gulls are common on the Vineyard.
The Herring Gull (*Larus argentatus*) adult has a white head and underparts. The wings are pale gray except for black tips. Legs and feet are pink, and the bill is yellow with a red spot. The Great Black-backed Gull (*Larus marinus*) is larger than the Herring Gull and has a black back in addition to black wings. The bill is the same as the Herring Gull.

59

Common Tern ©Michael Lane/123RF

Least Tern ©Raymond Hennessy/123RF

Terns

Sterna

Terns are more difficult to get to know than are gulls. They always stay right at the beach and are rarely, if ever, found in town or near people by choice. Terns may be distinguished from gulls by their pointed bill and wings and by their method of feeding; they plunge-dive into the water after fish. Two terns are common on the Vineyard. The Common Tern (*Sterna hirundo*) has a black head and gray wings. The underparts, including beneath the tail, are white. The bill is red and usually black-tipped. The Least Tern (*Sterna antillarum*) is smaller than the Common Tern and has a white forehead and yellow bill. Terns have a hard time reproducing because they often nest on the beach where they are disturbed by people and dogs. Great care should be taken not to disturb the nesting efforts of terns, not even "for just one picture."

Plovers
Charadrius

These compact birds dart across the ground, stop suddenly, then sprint off again. The Piping Plover (*Charadrius melodus*), a common type on the Vineyard, has pale brown upperparts and white underparts. Its legs are yellow, and it has a distinctive "peep-lo" call. Piping plovers build a pebble-lined nest right in the sand above high tide. Unfortunately, these nests are easily disturbed by beachgoers, and this has contributed to their decline.

©Raymond Hennessy/123RF

Cormorants
Phalacrocorax

Cormorants are large, dark water birds often seen sitting on buoys, where they spread their wings to dry them out. Their legs are short and stocky, and the neck is long.
Only the Double-crested Cormorant (*Phalacrocorax auritus*) is seen on the Vineyard in summer.
This cormorant can be recognized by its rounded orange throat pouch. Also, breeding adults have a double crest of two small tufts, curving back from behind the eyes.

©Mdf: CC BY-SA 3.0

SHELLS

While on a beach you may spot lots of shells. This nature guide discusses primarily those that were originally a protective covering for snails and bivalves (e.g., clams).

SNAILS

©Oleksandr Shpak/123RF

This photograph features a land snail (has lungs), but the snails whose shells are discussed in this section are sea snails, which have gills. The single shell of a snail coils about a central core that occasionally can be detected as a small opening known as the umbilicus. One complete spiral or twist of a snail shell is called a whorl. The first whorls to form are small and tightly coiled. Collectively called the spire, these small whorls are seen at the top of the shell. The later (lower) whorls are larger and broader. All snail shells have a large opening (the umbilicus), where the head and foot protrude.

Moon Shells

Typically, moon shells have four very small whorls and one very large whorl about the umbilicus, which looks like a deep hole. The shell of the Northern Moon Snail (*Lunatia heros*) is frequently found on the Vineyard. The shell is up to 3 inches in size and is delicately colored a pale yellow, tan, orange, or purple.

Moon snails are active predators. They dig through sand to find clams. They hold the clam with their foot and pierce the shell by using a toothy tongue (called the radula). Then they consume the organs of the clam.

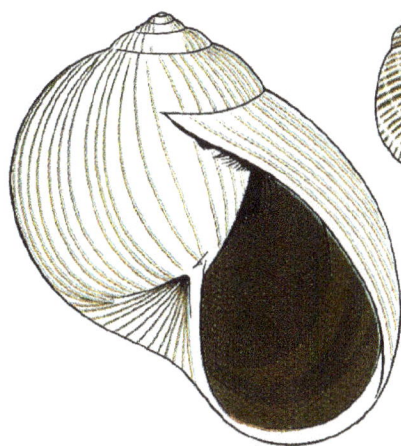
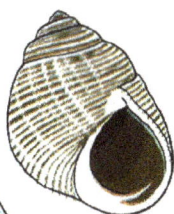

Periwinkle

Moon Snail   *Boat or Slipper Shell*

Periwinkle Shells

Periwinkle shells are small and conical. The common European Periwinkle (*Littorina littorea*) is typical of these shells. The smooth and thick shell is only 1/8 in. to 1 in. in size. It is grayish-brown to blackish, with a pattern of thin spiral lines alternating light and dark.

Periwinkles live on microscopic organisms that they scrape from the surface with their long, coiled radula (tongue). Some types can survive without water, and it is believed that land snails may have evolved from these.

Boat or Slipper Shells

A Boat Shell does not spiral like that of other snails. Instead, the overturned shell is cup-shaped and, if not too heavy, floats in water, accounting for the name—Boat Shell. In this position, you can also see a shelly platform covering about half the opening. The presence of this platform causes the shell to resemble a slipper.

The shell of the Common Atlantic Slipper (*Crepidula fornicata*) is usually up to 1½ inches in size. Most Atlantic Slipper Shells have a pattern of thin, reddish-brown lines, although some are dirty white or tan, without much color.

Whelk Shells

Whelk shells are beautifully whorled, with an opening along the elongated end. The Knobbed and Channeled Whelks are common on the Vineyard. Females lay long strings of egg capsules that are cemented to a stone or dead shell. These long strings are often found on the beach.

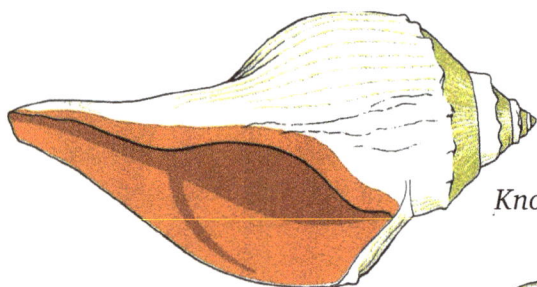

Knobbed Whelk

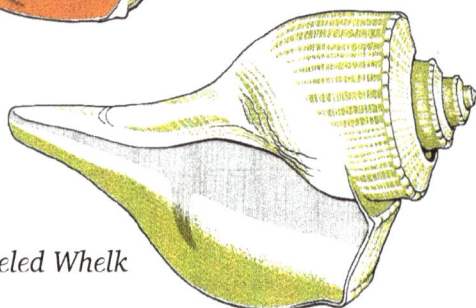

Channeled Whelk

The Knobbed Whelk (*Busycon carica*) can be up to 9 in. long. The shell of the adult is dirty gray, but the inside of the opening is a polished bright orange. There are distinct beadlike knobs on the outer edge (shoulder) of each whorl. The Channeled Whelk (*Busycon canaliculatum*) is up to 7 in. long. Its shell is light tan or gray-brown. The shoulders of the spire are angular rather than rounded; therefore, the spire appears to be a series of steps. There is a narrow channel that winds up the spire along the line where one whorl meets the next.

Whelks feed on hard-shelled clams. They use their foot to force the valves of the clam shell ajar. Then they wedge the edge of their shell between the clam's two valves and plunge a long proboscis deep into the soft parts of the clam.

Nassa Mud Snail

Atlantic Oyster Drill
©Bill Frank: CC BY-SA 4.0

Thick-lipped Drill
©Smithsonian Environmental
Research Center: CC BY-SA 2.0

Nassa Shells

Nassas shells are brownish and conical, with longitudinal ridges called ribs. In the shell of the Eastern Nassa Mud Snail (*Ilyanassa obsoleta*), common on the Vineyard, the intersection of spiral lines with the ribs gives the shell a beady appearance. This shell ranges in size from ½ to 1 inch; the color is variable, but is usually dark purple to red-brown. The opening is bordered on one side by enamel. These snails eat mud, gleaning organic matter from it as it is passed through the digestive tract.

Oyster Drill Shells

Oyster Drills are so named because they use their radula and a secretion of acid to make a hole in the shell of an oyster. Then they digest the organs of any oyster. In Oyster Drill shells, the ribs are deeper and the spiral lines are well defined. Both the Atlantic Oyster Drill (*Urosalpinx cinerea*) and the Thick-lipped Drill (*Eupleura caudata*) may be easily found on the Vineyard. Their brownish shell has five to six whorls, and there is a short canal below the oval opening. The outer lip of this opening tends to be thickened in the Atlantic Oyster Drill and quite thickened in the Thick-lipped Drill. There are usually about six teeth on this lip. Also, the whorls of the spire in the Thick-lipped Drill are angular rather than rounded.

BIVALVES

Clam Shell

©Yaroslav Domnitsky/123RF

Scallop Shell

©Olga Popova/123RF

The shell of clams and also scallops has two parts, or valves. Bivalves are filter feeders; they glean debris from the water that moves across their gills. Clams bury themselves in the sand after extending a large foot from the bottom of the open shell.

The shell of a scallop is flattened and looks like a fan because of its deep grooves. The projections to the sides of the narrow end are called "ears." The Atlantic Bay Scallop (*Argopecten irradians*) grows to a size of 2 to 3 in. Some shells have ridges that represent growth rings, formed in the spring when the animal resumes growing again. The live animal is able to quickly expel water from its mantle cavity so that it can swim rapidly away from a potential threat. It has thirty to forty bright-blue eyes along the outer opening of the shell.

Blue Mussel
©Pallbo: Public Domain

Atlantic Ribbed Mussel
©Andrew C: CC BY-SA 2.0

Mussel Shells

Most mussel shells are pear-shaped—the valves are much longer than they are wide.
The inside of each valve is shiny. The Blue Mussel (*Mytilus edulis*) and the Atlantic Ribbed Mussel (*Geukensia demissa*) are most often found on Vineyard beaches. These shells are about 3 in. long.

While you might expect the Blue Mussel to have a completely blue shell, this color is seen only wherever a shiny, varnishlike outer covering has worn away. Coarse, prominent growth lines are often present, but there are no ribs. The Atlantic Ribbed Mussel has a yellowish-brown shell, with numerous strong radiating ribs. The interior of the shell is bluish.

Clam Shells

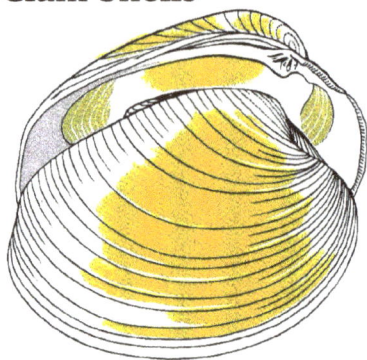

Northern Quahog

©Evelyn Jo Johnson

In the Northern Quahog (*Mercenaria mercenaria*) the hard, thick shell has a definite hump, with growth lines that become more definite toward the wider portion of the shell. As the clam matures to a size of about 4 in., a dark purple border develops on the inside of the shell. The Native Americans made purple wampum beads from this portion of the shell and used the beads as money. Large quahog clams are used on the Vineyard to make clam chowder. Little quahogs are known as little-neck clams. Littlenecks are steamed and eaten whole.

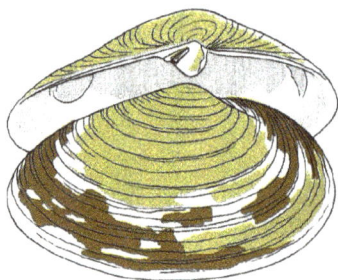

Soft-shell Clam

The Soft-shell Clam (*Mya arenaria*) can be up to 6 in. when grown. One valve of each pair has a hook at the hinge where the other valve attaches. This hook is affectionately known as a "nanny nose." The chalky-white shell, which may be concealed at least in part by a brownish covering, is oval, with one end somewhat more pointed than the other. This clam is also called the Long-necked Clam because it has siphons that are encased in a long tube that projects from the shell. Another name is Steamer Clam because steaming is the preferred method of cooking.

BEACHES

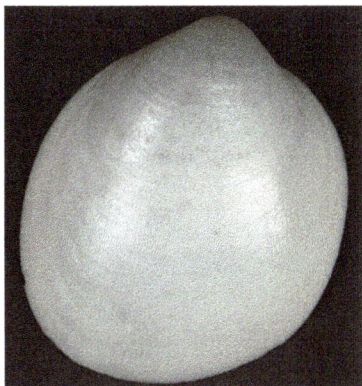

Egg cockle ©James St. John: CC BY-SA 2.0

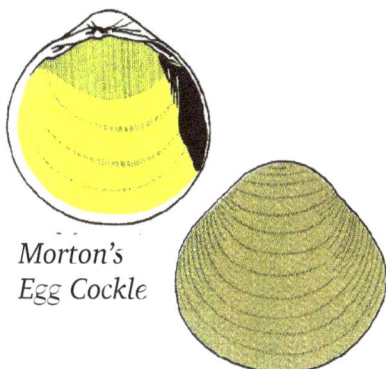

Morton's
Egg Cockle

Cockle Shells

Cockle shells are heart-shaped when viewed from top or bottom. Morton's Egg Cockle (*Laevicardium mortoni*) is the type of cockle most often seen on the beaches of the Vineyard. Up to 1 inch in length, the inside of the shell tends to be yellow, with a brown spot along one edge. The outside of the shell is usually light brownish.

©Evelyn Jo Johnson

Jingle Shell

Jingle Shells

Jingle Shells, which are related to oysters, have small translucent shells that range in size from ½ to 1¼ in. The Common Jingle (*Anomia simplex*) has a waxy luster, and the color varies from silver to yellow, orange, and black. One half of the shell is cup-shaped, and this is the half that usually washes ashore. The other half is flatter and has a hole through which strong threads pass to hold the animal to a rock or some other shell.

BEACHES

DUNES

Dunes are often located next to a beach. In addition to Beach Grass, there are other plants that can tolerate the sandy soil of the dunes. This section of our guide describes Beach Grass and the most common plants that grow on the back side of the dunes.

71

©Denis Tabler/ 123RF

GRASSES

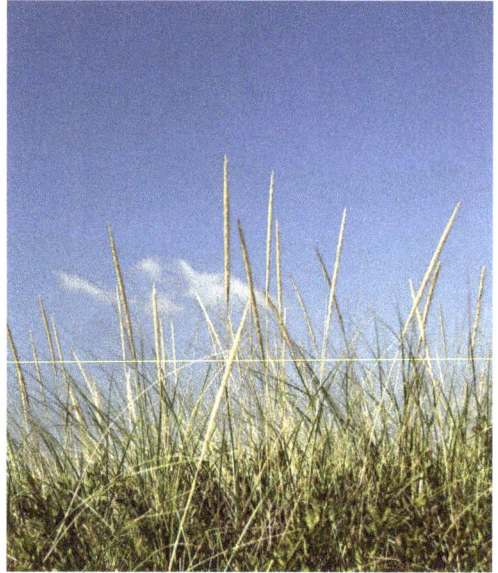

©Robhillphoto/123RF

Beach Grass
Ammophila breviligulata

Beach Grass is the grass found on the dunes. Although it looks quite sturdy, it is easily destroyed by the tramping of feet.

Therefore, to help preserve Vineyard beaches and dunes, it is better not to walk where there is Beach Grass. In some restored areas, the Beach Grass has been replanted, and in that case, it occurs in neat, parallel rows.

SHRUBS

©Famartin: CC BY-SA 4.0

Bayberry
Myrica pensylvanica

Bayberry is a spreading, much-branched shrub, with many oblong leaves that are 1 to 2 in. long. Its inconspicuous flowers are male or female. Only the female flowers develop into clusters of small, round, hard, white berries that adhere right to the stem and remain on the plant all winter. They are not edible except by birds. The berries were boiled by early settlers to get wax, from which they made fragrant bayberry candles. Because it takes so many berries to make even a small candle, today a fragrance is added to make candles smell like bayberry.

Flowers in spring. Berries in late summer and fall.

Beach Plum
Prunus maritima

The Beach Plum is a straggly, thornless shrub that stands 1 to 8 ft. tall. The oval, sharply toothed leaves are smooth on top and downy below.

Lovely white flowers bloom in early spring before the leaves are out.
These become the purple "plums" that are ½ to 1 in. in diameter. They ripen from August to October. Many famous Vineyard recipes feature this fruit, which can be used to make jellies and jams.

Flowers in spring. Fruit in late summer and fall.

Beach Pea
Lathyrus japonicus

The Beach Pea is a reclining plant that has branches as long as 4 to 5 ft. The leaves contain broad and blunt leaflets that can be paired or alternate.

The purple, sweet pea-shaped flowers are in long, stalked clusters that contain 3 to 10 flowers. Over time, these become pea pods.

Seaside Goldenrod
Solidago sempervirens

The Seaside Goldenrod is usually from 1 to 3 ft. in height. The alternate, toothless leaves, which often have some purplish pigment, are fleshy and able to hold water.

The yellow flowers are borne in a one-sided terminal cluster that is easily recognized as belonging to a goldenrod plant.

Flowers in fall.

Beach Wormwood or Dusty Miller
Artemisia stelleriana

A woolly gray, low-lying plant with deeply lobed leaves. This woolly-gray appearance is caused by a dusty that helps conserve water.

Small yellow flowers occur on central, upright stalks.

Flowers in summer.

©Evelyn Jo Johnson

Rosa Rugosa
Rosa rugosa

Rosa Rugosa (also called Beach Rose) is a shrub that grows from 2 to 6 ft. You are apt to find it along roadsides as well as on sandy dunes. The oval and oppo-sitely-placed leaves are so heavily wrinkled that the plant is sometimes called the Wrinkled Rose.

The large, singular flowers can be either deep-rose colored or white. In the fall, each flower becomes a large red hip, full of seeds. As with all rose hips, these are rich in vitamin C. Rosa Rugosa is one of the showiest plants on the Vineyard. You can easily learn to recognize it, both when it is flowering and when it has hips. Just keep in mind that the flowers and hips are large compared to other roses.

Flowers in spring. Hips in fall.

©Evelyn Jo Johnson

View of downtown Vineyard Haven from a ferry that is about to dock.

©Evelyn Jo Johnson

Nearby, sailboats dot the surface of the Vineyard Haven harbor.

SALTWATER MARSHES

Because the Vineyard is open to the sea at least occasionally, many of its ponds contain brackish water and are surrounded by grasses typical of a marsh. This section of our guide lists and describes these and other plants that can tolerate salty water.

79

©Jon Bilous/123RF

Grasses

Spartina

The grasses that grow in a salt marsh are of two types. One type, called Cordgrass (*Spartina alterniflora*), grows next to the water. It is stiff, has broad leaves, and grows in spikes that can easily cut bare feet.

A prevalent grass at the high-water line is a more delicate type that tends to bend over. This is called Saltmarsh Hay (*Spartina patens*) because the colonists harvested it to feed to their animals.

Cordgrass

Saltmarsh Hay

Glasswort
Salicornia virginica

This plant has a creeping, woody horizontal stem that gives off smooth, light-green, 4 to 12 in. jointed shoots. You often find it among the marsh grasses, particularly in areas that are not well drained. It is easier to detect in the fall when it turns bright red.

This is a flowering plant, but the minute flowers are inconspicuous and go unnoticed by most observers.

Flowers in late summer and early fall.

Sea Lavender
Limonium nashii

A 1 to 2-ft. high plant that has lance-shaped basal leaves that can be as long as 10 inches, as shown here.

The tiny (⅛ in.) flowers are pale purple and occur only on one side of the many branchlets. When a marsh is ringed by these plants, they give it a tinge of lavender color in the fall.

Flowers in late summer and early fall.

Groundsel Tree or High Tide Bush
Baccharis halimifolia

A shrub that grows from 3 to 6 ft. The alternate leaves are somewhat wedge-shaped and coarsely toothed.

The flowers are small and greenish and appear in clusters. Male and female flowers grow on different plants. In the fall, white-haired seeds mature on the female plant, causing the cluster to appear white and silky and very showy, as shown in the drawing.

Flowers in fall.

Swamp Marshmallow
Hibiscus palustris

A 2 to 4-ft. velvety, gray-green shrub. The leaves are heart-shaped or three-lobed. Cooking the root produces a sticky substance that originally was used in the making of marshmallows.

The showy pink flowers, each having five petals, are from 1 to 1½ in. wide. Each flower becomes a seed capsule in the fall.

Flowers from midsummer to early fall.

BIRDS
The birds listed under Wet Woodlands (p. 53) are also apt to be found on the waters of a saltwater marsh.

©Danny Kosmayer/123RF

Sunset at Gay Head Light. The Vineyard is famous for its beautiful sunsets.

OBSERVATIONS

CREDITS

WIKIPEDIA CREATIVE COMMONS/WIKIMEDIA COMMONS ATTRIBUTIONS

URLs for the following licenses:
CC BY-SA 2.0 https://creativecommons.org/licenses/by-sa/2.0/
CC BY-SA 2.5 https://creativecommons.org/licenses/by-sa/2.5/
CC BY-SA 3.0 https://creativecommons.org/licenses/by-sa/3.0/
CC BY-SA 4.0 https://creativecommons.org/licenses/by-sa/4.0/

MAP Page iv: Martha's Vineyard map by Norman Einstein taken 10/14/2005, license CC BY-SA 3.0 (added State Road, LCR (Lambert's Cove Road), and star to show location of lily pond).

OPEN FIELDS
p. 8: *Asclepias tuberosa* (butterfly weed) by Ragesoss, license CC BY-SA 3.0
p. 14: Pasture rose (Rosa Carolina) by D. Gordon E. Robertson, license CC BY-SA 3.0
p. 15: *Rosa multiflora* (whole plant, cropped) by Σ64, license CC BY-SA 3.0
p. 17: Dwarf sumac by Homer Edward Price, license CC BY-SA 2.0
p. 17: Smooth sumac by Eric Hunt: CC BY-SA 4.0
p. 19 (top): Poison ivy in May by Cramyourspam, license CC BY-SA 4.0
p. 19 (bottom): Poison ivy foliage during autumn by Famartin, license CC BY-SA 4.0
p. 23 (top, both): Red-tailed hawk and American kestrel (sparrow hawk) by Greg Hume (Greg5030), licenses CC BY-SA 3.0
p. 24 (both): American crow and American goldfinch by Mdf, licenses CC BY-SA 3.0
p. 25: Barn swallow by Malene Thyssen, license CC BY-SA 4.0
p. 25:Tree swallow by Iiii I I I, license CC BY-SA 4.0
p. 26: American robin by Kristof vt, license CC BY-SA 3.0
p. 26: Common starling by Fred Hsu, license CC BY-SA 3.0
p. 27 (bottom): Dove at Almaden Lake by Don DeBold, license CC BY-SA 2.0
p. 28: Bobwhite by BS Thurner Hoff, license CC BY-SA 3.0.

DRY WOODLANDS
p. 33: *Quercus velutina* (black oak, cropped) by Willow, license CC BY-SA 3.0
p. 33: Scarlet oak (cropped) by Famartin, license CC BY-SA 4.0
p. 34: Pitch pine trees (cropped) by Famartin, license CC BY-SA 3.0
p. 34: Red pine (cropped), by Rhododendrites, license CC BY-SA 4.0
p. 35: White pine cone by Keith Kanoti, Maine Forest Service, license CC BY-SA 3.0
p. 36: Sassafras by Wowbobwow12 at the English Language Wikipedia, license CC BY-SA 3.0
p. 39: Blue jay by Dick Daniels(http://carolinabirds.org), license CC BY-SA 3.0
p. 39: Rufous-sided towhee by Bill Thompson/US Fish & Wildlife Svc, Public Domain
p. 40: White-breasted nuthatch by www.naturespicsonline.com, license CC BY-SA 2.5
p. 40: Red-breasted nuthatch by Cephas, license CC BY-SA 3.0
p. 40: Black-capped chickadee by Mdf assumed, license CC BY-SA 3.0
p. 41: Brown thrasher family by cbgrfx123, license CC BY-SA 4.0
p. 41: Northern cardinal by Hari Krishnan, license CC BY-SA 4.0
p. 42: Downy woodpecker by Wolfgang Wander, license CC BY-SA 3.0
p. 42: Hairy woodpecker by Mdf, license CC BY-SA 3.0.

WET WOODLANDS
p. 46: Red maple (cropped) by Famartin, license CC BY-SA 4.0
p. 47: *Nyssa sylvatica* (beetlebung/tupelo tree, cropped) by Famartin, license CC BY-SA 4.0
p. 48: *Rhododendron viscosum* (Swamp azalea, cropped) by HorsePunchKid, license CC BY-SA 4.0
p. 49: Shadbush (flowers) by Fritzflohrreynolds, license CC BY-SA 3.0
p. 50: *Clethra alnifolia* (sweet pepperbush) by KENPEI, license CC BY-SA 3.0
p. 53: Red-winged blackbird by Walter Siegmund, license CC BY-SA 3.0
p. 53: Canada goose in Flight by Daniel D'Auria, license CC BY-SA 4.0
p. 55: Mallard by Richard Bartz, license CC BY-SA 2.5

BEACHES: SHORELINES
p. 59: *Larus argentatus*, Herring gull by Kurt Kulac, license CC BY-SA 4.0
p. 59: Great black-backed gull by Spinus Nature Photography: CC BY-SA 3.0
p. 61: Double-crested cormorant by Mdf, license CC BY-SA 3.0
p. 65: *Urosalpinx cinerea*, Atlantic oyster drill by Bill Frank, license CC BY-SA 4.0
p. 65: Thick-lipped drill by Smithsonian Environmental Research Center, license CC BY-SA 2.0
p. 67 (left, both): *Mytilus edulis* (blue mussel) by Pallbo: Public Domain;
p. 67: (right, both): Atlantic ribbed mussel (reoriented) by Andrew C., license CC BY-SA 2.0
p. 69: *Laevicardium* (egg cockle) by James St. John, license CC BY-SA 2.0.

BEACHES: DUNES
p. 73: Northern bayberry by Famartin, license CC BY-SA 4.0

INDEX

www.ingramcontent.com/pod-product-compliance
Lightning Source LLC
Chambersburg PA
CBHW051438270326
41931CB00019B/3470